TAR

Play Two of the trilogy
The Ballad of Bimini Baths

Tom Jacobson

BROADWAY PLAY PUBLISHING INC
New York
www.broadwayplaypub.com
info@broadwayplaypub.com

TAR

Cover photo: Playwrights' Arena

First edition: August 2018
I S B N: 978-0-88145-791-9

Book design: Marie Donovan
Page make-up: Adobe InDesign
Typeface: Palatino

TAR was originally produced by Playwrights' Arena (Jon Lawrence Rivera, Artistic Director; Henry "Heno" Fernandez, Producer), premiering on 9 June 2018. The cast and creative contributors were:

ZENOBIO .... Adrian Gonzalez
AMEN .... Noel Arthur
DONALD .... Tim Ryan Meinelschmidt

Director .... Edgar Landa
Set designer .... Justin Huen
Costume designer .... Mylette Nora
Lighting designer .... Derek Jones
Sound designer .... Howard Ho
Stage manager .... Leticia Chang
Casting director .... Raul Staggs

CHARACTERS & SETTING

ZENOBIO REMEDIOS, *36, a bathing attendant*
AMEN HEADLEY, *20s–30s, a bathing attendant*
DONALD WALTER, *30s–50s, an unemployed secretary*

The action takes place in a storage area in Bimini Baths in Los Angeles.

An October evening in 1939.

The storage room has a lot of junk, including outdated and little-used bathing equipment. The only new equipment is a Dictaphone. Blue and green light from the neon sign next door shines into the room through high windows. Two doors, one interior and one exterior.

SPECIAL THANKS

Joy Meads, Patricia Garza, Pier Carlo Talenti, Center Theatre Group's L A Writers' Workshop, Son of Semele Ensemble, Lois Arkin, L A Eco Village, Betty Uyeda, John Cahoon, Brent Riggs, Dr William Estrada, Seaver Center for Western History Research, Stan Yogi, Cathy McNassor, Kibo Desoto Knight

(A body lies under a sheet on a table, one brown arm exposed. AMEN HEADLEY, *20s-30s, dressed in an attendant's uniform, gazes up at the green and blue neon light filtering into the room through high windows.* ZENOBIO REMEDIOS, *36, also dressed as an attendant, struggles with a Dictaphone.)*

ZENO: *(Into the Dictaphone) Hola, buenas dias… (Plays it back) Este es* Zenobio Remedios— *(Plays it back)*

AMEN: You need help with that? Stupid new procedure—

ZENO: No!

AMEN: Amen never used a Dictaphone before either, but I bet I can—

*(*ZENO *plays it back: "No!")*

AMEN: I see, I see. Suit yourself, Zeno.

ZENO: Quiet! It's recording. *(Into the Dictaphone) Mi nombre es Zeno—*

AMEN: *(Into the Dictaphone)* Zeno the beanbag.

ZENO: Amen, I'm trying to—

AMEN: Zeno the greaser.

ZENO: Shut up, you damn—

AMEN: Say it!

ZENO: No!

*(*ZENO *struggles with the Dictaphone.* AMEN *speaks into it.)*

AMEN: Spic.

ZENO: Shhh!

AMEN: *(Whispers)* Spic.

ZENO: Spook.

AMEN: Wetback.

ZENO: Spade.

AMEN: Pachuco.

ZENO: Dinge.

AMEN: Mojado.

*(*ZENO *hesitates.)*

AMEN: *(Gleeful)* Say it! You wanna say it!

ZENO: *(After a moment)* Golliwog!

AMEN: Aw! Spiggoty!

ZENO: *(Laughs)* Spiggoty?

AMEN: Spiggoty English?

ZENO: Chango!

AMEN: Chango?

ZENO: Spiggoty Spanish, eight ball?

AMEN: Beaner!

ZENO: You said that already. I win.

AMEN: *(Overlapping)* I said beanbag.

ZENO: Maroon!

AMEN: Border nigger.

ZENO: You said it! I win.

AMEN: Amen used a modifier, an *adjective.* It ain't the same. Mojo.

*(*ZENO *can't think of anything.)*

AMEN: *(Helpfully)* Coon, buck, July ham?

ZENO: Smoked Irish!

AMEN: Chihuahua!

ZENO: Chihuahua? *(Thinks)*

AMEN: *(Helpfully)* Shine, haunt, blue gum?

ZENO: Blue gum?

AMEN: If you get bit by a Negro with blue gums, you die. Thirty- Eighth Streeter!

(ZENO *can't think of anything.)*

AMEN: Say it!

ZENO: I'm not saying—

AMEN: Go on, say it!

ZENO: George!

AMEN: Damn!

ZENO: *(Laughing)* Don't get sore, George!

AMEN: Call me a smoke or a dinge or Monsieur Midnight or Sir Inky but don't be such a damn fool to call me George!

ZENO: Your game. I just play better'n you—George.

AMEN: You sure know how to kick a fellow! That's the lousiest, phoniest, countriest—

ZENO: *(Back to working the Dictaphone)* Enough—epithets!

AMEN: Epithets!

ZENO: You're distracting me again. We gotta get to work—	AMEN: Ain't that what goes on a tomb? Ep-i-thet!

AMEN: Always get the shit work.

ZENO: Always?

ZENO: You been working here two weeks—	AMEN: Who gets the nastiest—?

ZENO: I asked for—

AMEN: You asked for this mess—?

ZENO: I know how to do it—no one else has the technique—

AMEN: Well, I didn't ask!

ZENO: I asked for you.

AMEN: You hate Amen that bad?

ZENO: It's a strange situation—

AMEN: We're a bath house, not a morgue—

ZENO: You goofball, he's not—	AMEN: —Not a hospital—
ZENO: —It's an opportunity—	AMEN: —Not a goddam funeral home!

ZENO: —We can both look good, impress Mr Warrick— *(Gets control of the Dictaphone)* There!

AMEN: I see, I see. So we get promoted to what? Senior Ass-Wipe?

ZENO: *(Into Dictaphone)* October 2, 1939—

AMEN: Hind Tit Brigade?

ZENO: Bimini Hot Springs and Resort treatment log, Medical Division.

*(*ZENO *rifles through a pile of dirty clothes.)*

AMEN: Forty years ago, my daddy owned this land.

ZENO: *(Finds a wallet)* My daddy owns Hollywoodland—

AMEN: Spent his life savings on the acreage and an oil rig—

ZENO: Subject is one— *(Reading from wallet)* —Donald Walter.

AMEN: —And lost it all when he struck mineral water instead—

ZENO: Victim is male, approximately— *(Looks at body under sheet)*

ZENO: Fifty years of age.

AMEN: He had to sell to Doctor Edwards at a loss—

AMEN: —And Edwards built the baths that paid for themselves within a year—

ZENO: Mr Walter appears to have suffered trauma to—

AMEN: While my daddy died without a penny to his name.

ZENO: Will you shut up? I'm trying to record!

AMEN: Shut up, what? Shut up, nnnnnnnnnn—

ZENO: Shut up, you—fffffffabulist! *(Into Dictaphone)* —Suffered an accident when—

AMEN: Ooh, *fabulist*!

ZENO: I give up. Screw documentation procedure!

AMEN: What's a fabulist?

(ZENO abandons the Dictaphone.)

ZENO: A fabulist is a liar, a spinner of stories—

AMEN: A liar?!

ZENO: A teller of tall tales— *(He starts preparing cloths, brushes and a can of kerosene to work on the body.)*

AMEN: Ain't no tall tale! Amen ain't no liar.

ZENO: *(Demonstrating)* Take a cloth—

AMEN: My daddy not only owned the lot for Bimini Baths—

(ZENO wets the cloth with kerosene and starts cleaning the body under the sheet. AMEN follows ZENO's instructions as he talks. They clean the body together, concentrating on the legs.)

AMEN: —He owned the land under Charles Ray Studios where Mr Ray shot *The Courtship of Miles Standish*, starring himself as Miles Standish—

ZENO: Gently, gotta be respectful—

AMEN: —With a full scale replica of the Mayflower on a lake in the middle of the lot—

AMEN: Like he's gonna care!

*(*ZENO *hands* AMEN *the wallet.* AMEN *puts it back in the clothes.)*

ZENO: *(Cleaning)* This is gonna come off in layers—

*(*AMEN *holds up a switchblade he found in the clothes. He clicks it open.)*

ZENO: Put that back! It ain't yours!

AMEN: *(Puts knife back in clothes)* Police didn't search him too good.

ZENO: You wanna get accused of stealing? We're on thin ice with Warrick as it is—

AMEN: *(Looking under the sheet)* What the fuck happened to this raggedy chump?!

ZENO: An awful accident—

AMEN: How does that even—?

AMEN: *(Sniffs)* Musta been splifficated—look at his skin—!

ZENO: That's what we gotta fix. Clean him up.

AMEN: Damn.

ZENO: Respectfully.

AMEN: Amen gotta take a break.

ZENO: We just started, you lazy—

AMEN: Nnnnnnnn—!

ZENO: Nnnnnnnot saying it.

AMEN: *(Staring at the neon)* I respect that. I do. And I thank you for trying to advance Amen with opportunities for extra work—

ZENO: You're welcome—

AMEN: Even if it's work for a goddamn body servant—

ZENO: That's what we do here! We're a luxury resort! We take care of personal needs, no matter how—unusual—

AMEN: *(Lighting a cigarette)* No offense. Truly! You're a good boss. Amen apologizes for his insufficient gratitude—

ZENO: Then get over here and help me! *(Sees cigarette)*

AMEN: My daddy even owned the land— *(Gestures toward neon lights)* —Under the Palomar Ballroom.

ZENO: *(Grabbing* AMEN*)* Stub out that gasper!

ZENO: *(Stubbing out the cigarette)* This is kerosene, you stupid—	AMEN: Hands off, you grabby thing!

(Behind them, the body stirs.)

AMEN: Nnnnnnnn—!

ZENO: You wanna fry this bum and scorch us with him!?

AMEN: Amen was joking with the ciggy.

ZENO: That kinda joke's not just a joke. There's consequences.

*(*AMEN *and* ZENO *clean the body.)*

AMEN: And epithets! Consequences and epithets! What're we using kerosene for, anyways? That can't be good for the complexion.

ZENO: It's an oil-based solvent—the only thing that works on tar.

AMEN: He tarred and feathered?

ZENO: That doesn't happen in California.

AMEN: Mmm-hmmm.

ZENO: You see any feathers?

AMEN: Maybe he got plucked.

AMEN: Got plucked up! ZENO: You need to take this serious.

ZENO: What if you lose your job and they start up the draft?

AMEN: We ain't in Poland.

ZENO: A month ago, neither were the Nazis. Unemployed colored men'll be first pick for the front lines, so we gotta play by the rules. When Warrick hired you, he said you told him you had a work ethic.

AMEN: I keep it next to my epithet.

ZENO: He's looking for someone to take charge of Mechanotherapy, and if I get that position, maybe you'll get mine. If you toe the line.

AMEN: They ain't never gonna promote a Chihuahua or a nnnnnnnnn—

ZENO: If we get in the war, everything's gonna change. They'll need manpower—won't matter if I'm Spanish—

AMEN: Spanish!? That what you call yourself?

ZENO: It's what I speak.

AMEN: With a Mexican accent. Where'd you say your daddy's from?

ZENO: Oaxaca. San Pedro Huamelula.

AMEN: No one from Ha cha cha Watch-me-lula's gonna head up the Mechanotherapy department. We can't even use the plunge on our days off!

ZENO: Yes, we can—

AMEN & ZENO: —Once a month!

AMEN: On Mexican Day! The day before we clean the pool.

ZENO: I'm just saying, be respectful, be diligent, and we'll both at least have a chance.

AMEN: Courtesy is an act of kindness, or a duty performed with politeness.

ZENO: Uh…yeah…

AMEN: One who is always courteous merely shows in a natural way his wish to be kind.

ZENO: Where'd you get that?

AMEN: Employees should study how to help all patrons to use the cars—

ZENO: Ah!

AMEN: —So they may enjoy the advantages of all conveniences offered and obtain the maximum benefit therefrom.

ZENO: Therefrom!

AMEN: Therefrom my epithet!

ZENO: So you know how to be respectful—

AMEN: There's two versions of Amen: one for work—when there's pecks watching—and one for play, when they ain't.

ZENO: You're just playing a role.

AMEN: Amen is a professional actor! And you are, too, you just don't know it. Señor Remedios need to get him some race consciousness. What you gonna do with a promotion, anyhow?

ZENO: Saving for school.

AMEN: School for what?

ZENO: Paleontology.

AMEN: The study of pale people?

ZENO: Prehistoric animals. Like from the Tar Pits: sabertooth tigers and mammoths and giant ground sloths—

AMEN: Tar Pits? You mean like this—? *(Indicates body)*

ZENO: When I was a kid I learned to clean the tar off the bones at the Museum. *(Pulls out a small brown bone)*

AMEN: What's that?

ZENO: A bacculum.

AMEN: English!

ZENO: A penis bone.

AMEN: Human?

ZENO: From a dire wolf.

AMEN: I'd be pretty damn dire if you stole my dick.

ZENO: It's from the Tar Pits!

AMEN: You stole a dick bone from the Tar Pits?

ZENO: *(Shoving it back in his pocket)* No!

AMEN: And you keep it in your pocket?

(Off ZENO*'s look)*

AMEN: Don't be embarrassed. Used to have me a rabbit's foot.

ZENO: It's an artifact! Prehistoric!

AMEN: I see, I see. You living in the past, in a museum with dead things where nothing happen, nothing moves.

ZENO: I'm saving for school, for my future!

AMEN: They teach that pale shit at Santa Monica Junior College?

ZENO: Yale University.

AMEN: Yale University! *(Laughs)* Señor Remedios going to Yale! Now who's the fabulist?

ZENO: You could go to college, too, if you save up.

AMEN: Amen is an autodidact.

ZENO: You don't even have a car.

AMEN: I'm self-taught! How long you been saving? Seem like you gonna be the world's oldest freshman—and maybe the darkest— Spanishest—

ZENO: Shut up and clean, you dumb-ass nnnnegro!

AMEN: *(Jubilant)* Amen almost got you! You right next door to saying it!

ZENO: I will not be provoked to prejudice.

AMEN: Stubbornness. That's what you got.

ZENO: Courtesy is an act of kindness.

AMEN: Now you poking fun at Amen. That ain't so kind.

ZENO: Amen, you're not a fool however much you act it. Be serious. You gotta be serious about something.

AMEN: Serious? Shit!

ZENO: You gotta want something. What is it?

AMEN: As a professional actor, I must maintain an air of mystery.

ZENO: Bushwa!

AMEN: What good's wanting do? Never gonna get it.

ZENO: I wanted this job and I got it. Didn't you want this job?

AMEN: Yeah.

ZENO: And you got it.

AMEN: You talked Warrick into it.

(ZENO *shrugs.)*

AMEN: You embarrassed! You embarrassed that you nice!

*(*AMEN *and* ZENO *clean in silence for a while.)*

AMEN: Know what Amen want?

ZENO: Something ridiculous.

AMEN: I wanna see Count Basie play at the Palomar.

ZENO: Mm-hmm, ridiculous.

AMEN: I hear him on the radio, saw him at the Dunbar Hotel, Club Alabam—and now—for the first time—*(Gestures to blue and green light)* —His name in lights at the Palomar Ballroom!

ZENO: Progress! Maybe someday they'll let you in.

AMEN: He's playing there tonight! The first Negro ever!

ZENO: Too bad we have to work.

AMEN: We get off at ten.

ZENO: Go chase yourself.

AMEN: The Palomar will be chock full of women.

ZENO: White women.

AMEN: Ain't that at least a little intriguing to you?

ZENO: Exactly why we can't get in.

AMEN: You want protection from the evil white chicks, no worry, Amen'll be with you.

ZENO: Not the women I'm worried about.

AMEN: You can't dance?

ZENO: I dance some.

AMEN: Palomar's the best dancing west of Central Avenue.

ZENO: Amen, you rascal—

AMEN: You shy? Around women?

ZENO: Awkward, maybe.

AMEN: Awkward? A Valentino like you? You a punk?

ZENO: Shut up.

AMEN: You scared of being refused.

ZENO: I'm more like to pass than you.

AMEN: They'll think you're high yellow.

ZENO: I hate being humiliated.

AMEN: You think we gonna get all togged up, pretend we a couple of paddies and talk our way through the front door? *(Opens the door)* Naw, man, I got a secret way into the joint. Hey, will you listen to that?

(Music pours in through the open door from the Palomar Ballroom across the street. It's the last few bars of Roseland Shuffle.)

AMEN: *(Dances a few steps)* It's *Roseland Shuffle*! We gotta get in there!

ZENO: Amen, back to work! Secret way or not, we'd get kicked out—

AMEN: Not if we had—hey! His togs! *(He starts rifling through the pile of clothes as the song ends.)*

AMEN: Not like he needs his driver's license tonight—

*(*ZENO *wrestles the clothes and wallet away from* AMEN*. Behind them, the body under the sheet stirs.)*

ZENO: Are you some kinda weed-head? Get out of there! We could get in a real mess!

(Another song starts up: Taxi War Dance. AMEN *runs to the door.)*

ZENO straightens the clothes.

AMEN: That's *Taxi War Dance*! The Count's best song of 1939!

ZENO: Back to the kerosene!

*(*ZENO *finds something in the pocket of the pants he is straightening. It looks like a shiny piece of flexible black rubber a few inches long. He stares at it.* AMEN *dances a little as he stares out at the green and blue neon.)*

AMEN: Let's just lock up and go! I know the fellows in the kitchen.

ZENO: *(Confused)* What the hell?

AMEN: They'll let us in the service entrance!

AMEN: We can watch the show back stage—maybe even meet Count Basie—-slip right by them peckerwoods!

*(*ZENO *wraps a handkerchief around the rubber object and shoves it into his pocket before* AMEN *sees it. Behind them, the body under the sheet stirs more.)*

ZENO: Close the door!

AMEN: This is historic! Don't just sit around watching your whole life! Time to get out and *do*!

ZENO: Get back to work!

AMEN: Count Basie's first night at the Palomar! Progress!

*(*AMEN *grabs* ZENO.*)*

ZENO: You crazy monkey!

AMEN: At least let's dance!

*(*AMEN *starts dancing with* ZENO. *It's awkward at first as* ZENO *resists and each struggles to lead.)*

AMEN: Come on, daddy-o! I bet you're a secret floorflusher!

ZENO: Cut it out, Amen!

AMEN: Shake your stilts! We got a job to do!

*(*AMEN *forces* ZENO *to reveal he can dance quite well.)*

ZENO: It's not respectful!

AMEN: Get hot! Get hot!

ZENO: I'm nothing but a heeler!

ZENO: If Warrick catches us—!

AMEN: No you ain't! You got it!

AMEN: He went home!

*(*ZENO *surrenders to the dancing.* AMEN *and* ZENO *are both excellent and dance well together. It's free, joyful.)*

AMEN: Now you're on the trolley!

*(*AMEN *and* ZENO *dance with more and more exuberance, quite a show. Behind them, the sheet is thrown off by* DONALD WALTER, *a white man stained by asphalt up to his chin. He is partially clothed. He stares at* AMEN *and* ZENO *dancing together and is confused, still drunk. He sees his own dark arms, holds them up, staring.)*

DONALD: *Was ist passiert?* [What's happened?] *(New Jersey accent)* I turned! I turned!

*(*AMEN *and* ZENO *stop dancing immediately.* ZENO *rushes to* DONALD.*)*

AMEN: He ain't dead!

ZENO: Mr Walter, you're okay!

DONALD: I knew it would happen! They said I'd turn!

ZENO: We're gonna take care of you!

AMEN: He's a goddamn zombie!

DONALD: *Gott im Himmel!* [God in heaven!]

AMEN: Don't show him no salt or he'll kill you to get back to his grave!

DONALD: Who're you?

ZENO: I'm Zeno and this is Amen.

AMEN: Don't touch him, Zeno! It's contagious!

DONALD: Contagious!

ZENO: Stop acting a fool! You knew he was just passed out!

DONALD: That's what they said! Where are we?

AMEN: Bimini Baths and Hot Springs Resort—

DONALD: Is that where they send 'em? I hear race music—

(ZENO closes the door, shutting out the band music.)

AMEN: Send who? The zombies?

DONALD: The coloreds! Is that why they sent me here? Cause I turned?

(AMEN and ZENO look at each other, puzzled.)

ZENO: Mr Walter, we're here to clean you up—

DONALD: You're here same reason I am.

AMEN: Cause we're colored?

DONALD: They always said if you fuck coloreds, you turn colored, too—

AMEN: Who said?

ZENO: No, Mr Walter, you're just—

DONALD: Everybody knows—did you fuck coloreds?

ZENO: You had an accident—

AMEN: If that was true, every ofay master in Dixie'd be black as midnight—

DONALD: It's like the clap, the lues—

AMEN: *(Giggling)* The syph! The pox! The drip!

ZENO: Amen, act professional!

AMEN: Brother Walter, lemme ask you: you pissing pins and needles?

DONALD: That a symptom?

AMEN: Maybe. But it seem like you got the biggest symptom of all: *(Indicates* DONALD*'s arms)* You got you some shade.

ZENO: Amen, don't—he's still blotto—

AMEN: *(Winks at* ZENO*)* It's rare, but it happens. Now that we brothers—

DONALD: *Scheisse!* Oh, shit! Shit!

AMEN: I'm a help you piece together the circumstances of your…racelift.

DONALD: I can't… ZENO: Jesus, Amen!

AMEN: No shame in it. Happens to the best and the brightest. You have you some intimate relations with the darker races and it's only natural that a little rubs off. Thank God for segregation or the whole country'd be corked up by now.

DONALD: But…I didn't—

AMEN: There are other ways this can occur. You eat anything overcooked or burnt?

DONALD: I don't think so.

AMEN: Any other kind of exposure to darkness?

DONALD: I don't wanna say.

AMEN: How we gonna help you if you don't—?

DONALD: You can help me?

ZENO: It's our job to help you— DONALD: Lighten me again? I can come back?

AMEN: We can't do nothing for you less we know the truth. What'd you do, Donald?

ZENO: You don't have to say, Mr. Walter.

DONALD: It ain't permanent?

ZENO: No, it's just—

AMEN: It turns permanent if you wait too long. I did.

DONALD: You…turned?

AMEN: I did.

DONALD: How?

AMEN: It's different for everybody. I'll tell you my story once you fess up about yours…brother.

DONALD: Can't think of nothing.

AMEN: Yes, you can. Don't let embarrassment stand in the way of your cure. You let this go on more than an hour, it'll stick.

DONALD: Okay, okay, it might've been the shrimping.

AMEN: You don't say? Shrimping?

DONALD: In Ballona Creek, still some shrimp in the estuary even after the concrete went in—

ZENO: *(Pulling* AMEN *aside)* Amen, don't lead him down this path!

*(*DONALD *is so drunk he continues his story even when they step away.)*

DONALD: —You can get 'em when the tide comes in—

AMEN: He'll figure it out soon enough, but I wanna play this cracker a little—

ZENO: When he sobers up, he's gonna tell Warrick you played him—

AMEN: He gonna be too ashamed to complain. Too humiliated.

DONALD: The mud there is deep, with a shallow layer of water on top.

ZENO: This job might mean shit to you, but it's everything to me.

AMEN: We are slaves here, Zeno. Glorified house niggers!

ZENO: Amen, I'm your boss you're talking to!

DONALD: And you can sink in up to your chest before you know it with just your head sticking out of the water—

AMEN: You ain't the boss so much as flunky overseer!

DONALD: And the mud's so thick, like pudding, like, like, Vaseline—

ZENO: I'm sorry you feel that way, Amen, I truly am.

DONALD: The smell's strong, a powerful mud smell, got me hard—

AMEN: Aw, Zeno, you're cool, I don't wanna hurt your—

DONALD: Just the smell, but then the feel of the mud, the ooze and thickness, like cream—

ZENO: You are! You're hurting my chances and your own!

DONALD: Up to my teats in mud—

AMEN: I see, I see.

AMEN: What's he talking about, teats?

DONALD: Strong black mud like a dark pussy swallowing my legs, my dick—

DONALD: —Sliding up the crack of my ass—

ZENO: Get him off of this and tell him the truth!

DONALD: I shoved my trunks full of mud, got me harder and harder—

AMEN: He's so deep I don't know I can pull him out!

DONALD: Couldn't breathe the mud was so tight around my chest,

ZENO: So stinko he can hardly see!

gasping, my chin sticking out of the water—

DONALD: Never been so hard! Then I jizzed the mud, exploded in my trunks—

AMEN: I gotta do it gradual or—

DONALD: I was covered! Covered in thick, black— *(Rubs arms)* That what this is?

DONALD: Did it get in me and leak back out?

ZENO: It's tar.

ZENO: You're covered in tar. *(Into Dictaphone)* Subject has recovered consciousness—

AMEN: You our little tar baby.

DONALD: *(Re: Dictaphone)* That's the wrong button— you gotta—

ZENO: Hush, Amen!

DONALD: When I was a secretary, I used—

AMEN: And it could well be forever.

DONALD: Forever?

ZENO: *(Abandons Dictaphone)* It's not forever! We're cleaning you, if you'll just hold still—

AMEN: Oh, I don't know. There been cases.

DONALD: I want a mirror! Please get me a mirror!

ZENO: *(Looking for a mirror)* Sure—

AMEN: *(Stopping* ZENO*)* Naw, might be too much of a shock. You gotta get used to the idea before you see the evidence on your face. Took me several weeks to settle in.

(Off DONALD*'s look)*

AMEN: I used to be white as you. The old you. White as you were.

DONALD: How'd you turn?

AMEN: Well, like you said, intimate relations.

DONALD: Intimate relations?

ZENO: *(Pulling* AMEN *aside)* Jesus, Amen!

(As they confer, AMEN *holds his hand on the small of* ZENO*'s back as he did when they were dancing.)*

DONALD: How many times?

AMEN: He won't remember none of this in the morning.

DONALD: Who was it?

ZENO: We'll both get fired if you keep messing with him!

DONALD: Hey.

AMEN: I'll get him a mirror in a little bit. But lemme have my fun first.

ZENO: Might have to fire you myself.

AMEN: Fire me?

DONALD: Hey!

ZENO: Warrick heard about you and the colonic flush—

AMEN: I never gave one before—!

DONALD: Hey…brothers?

*(*AMEN *and* ZENO *look at* DONALD.*)*

DONALD: Were you…*dancing*?

*(*AMEN *and* ZENO *go back to cleaning* DONALD.*)*

AMEN: Naw, man, you drunk, hallucinating.

ZENO: See?!

DONALD: I ain't drunk. I ain't drunk. Two men dancing—

AMEN: You ain't drunk, you ossified! Be patient and we'll get you all fixed up.

ZENO: That's right, Mr. Walter, just relax.

AMEN: But before we do, we're obligated to inquire: you absolutely convinced you wish to be white again?

DONALD: Yes!

AMEN: For sure and certain? I chose to become Negro—weren't no accident.

DONALD: You chose? Why?

ZENO: Amen, help me get his shirt off.

AMEN: Why? I'm a little shocked you'd even ask that, Brother Donald.

*(*AMEN *and* ZENO *peel his tar-sticky shirt off of him slowly. His skin is stained dark beneath.)*

AMEN: It's due to the advantages.

DONALD: The advantages of being colored?

AMEN: The privileges!

DONALD: What privileges?

AMEN: The majority of Americans are white, yes?

DONALD: Yes…

AMEN: So the majority uses the white water fountain. That's a lot of people. A lot of germs. By using the colored fountain, we're sharing among a smaller, elite group, thereby limiting—

AMEN: —The likelihood of disease.

ZENO: Thereby!

AMEN: You ever gone to see a movie and it's so crowded you have to sit in the front row, your neck craning and your eyes so close to the screen you're almost blinded?

DONALD: Yeah.

AMEN: The colored section in the balcony is at a safe distance, minimizing eye strain and preventing cataracts in later life. That's why they call it paradise.

DONALD: Uh-huh.

AMEN: And I don't have to tell you once you turn Negro your masculine capacities are considerably more…capacious.

DONALD: *(Half-heartedly pawing at his crotch)* I can't—

ZENO: Amen, that's enough.

AMEN: Being *Spanish*, Zeno's not all the way black—

AMEN: —But he can tell you what it's like to be a Latin lover like Rudolph Valentino, catnip to the kittens.

ZENO: Amen, more kerosene and less bushwa—

AMEN: And although U S law guarantees the right to a speedy trial, we all seen legal proceedings that go on and on. You ever notice who is forced to suffer through those long trials?

DONALD: Who?

AMEN: White folks! Black folks not only save the trouble of a jury trial but also the expense of a lawyer—we skip straight to justice on the nearest lynching tree.

ZENO: Don't pay his nonsense any attention, Mr Walter—

DONALD: Um…

AMEN: Those are but a few of the privileges of color, Brother Donald.

DONALD: And music.

AMEN: Music?

DONALD: Race music. My wife thinks it's hot.

AMEN: She prefer brass or wood?

DONALD: What?

AMEN: Trumpet, sax or clarinet?

DONALD: Not clarinet. Definitely not clarinet!

AMEN: I love me some Lester Young—

DONALD: No clarinet!

AMEN: You like Count Basie?

DONALD: I like opera.

ZENO: Amen.

AMEN: Opera! *(To ZENO)* Scrub harder!

DONALD: On the radio. Vivian got in the chorus of the Wagner Festival at the Hollywood Bowl.

AMEN: She sings?

DONALD: Don't talk about my wife.

AMEN: Do you sing?

DONALD: *I* get to talk about Vivian.

DONALD: We came out to Hollywood when she got in a movie. Sang in some amateur productions. She got lots of opera boys.

Popular—and beautiful! Hypnotic on screen. *(To ZENO)* You ever seen a woman like that in real life? Hypnotic?

ZENO: Sure.

AMEN: Clara Bow, Fredi Washington, Nina Mae McKinney.

DONALD: That's Vivian. Face and voice. You understand, Zeno?

AMEN: Theresa Harris, Ethel Moses— I met 'em all.

ZENO: I do.

DONALD: A kiss from her is a kiss from heaven. Like an angel's kissing you.

ZENO: She sounds nice.

DONALD: When she kisses you, you know you're loved.

AMEN: That's some kiss.

DONALD: Not everybody appreciates a woman like that.

ZENO: Which movie?

DONALD: What?

ZENO: Which movie was Mrs Walter in, may I ask?

DONALD: A western. *Eyes of the Totem.*

ZENO: You don't say! Who'd she play?

AMEN: I'm an actor, too.	DONALD: Little role, a student.

ZENO: In the seminary?

AMEN: I had a couple of movie roles.	DONALD: You saw *Eyes of the Totem*?

ZENO: I like westerns. That the one where the lady leads a double life as a beggar and a member of society while putting her daughter through private seminary?

DONALD: Set in Tacoma.

AMEN: Tacoma's nice.	DONALD: We didn't go. It was just a set.

AMEN: Not as nice as Seattle, of course.

DONALD: Vivian's a soprano.

AMEN: Where're you from, Brother Donald?	DONALD: She's sung Sieglinde and Brunnhilde.

AMEN: Did I hear you speaking German earlier?

DONALD: My mother's from Sudetenland.

AMEN: And am I detecting a New York accent?

DONALD: It's Jersey!

AMEN: Ah, the Garden State.

DONALD: You've been?

AMEN: Amen traveled to every state in our union.

DONALD: All forty-eight?

AMEN: And most of Mexico. I don't believe in sitting around. I gotta move! I gotta *do*!

DONALD: I been to maybe a dozen states.

ZENO: I never left California!

AMEN: How are we to know our great country without we traverse its length and breadth?

ZENO: Traverse!

AMEN: As a professional actor, I want to tell the story of America, the whole story, all the states, so I made it my business to visit all.

ZENO: Professional actor!

DONALD: Every damn state. I can't believe it.

AMEN: I am indeed!

ZENO: What've you been in?

DONALD: Doesn't seem right…

AMEN: I am a trained Shakespearean.

ZENO: On the Chitlin Ciruit!

DONALD: How'd you afford all those trips?

AMEN: With lead roles!

AMEN: As a professional actor, I maintain an air of mystery.

ZENO: Let's hear some Shakespeare then.

AMEN: *(English accent)* He hath disgraced me, and hindered me half a million; laughed at my losses, mocked at my gains, scorned my nation, thwarted my bargains, cooled my friends, heated mine enemies; and what's his reason? I am a Negro. Hath not a Negro eyes? Hath not a Negro hands, organs, dimensions, senses, affections, passions?

DONALD: No. No, no!

AMEN: Fed with the same food—

DONALD: You can't—that's not—!

AMEN: Hurt with the same weapons, subject to the same diseases, healed by the same means, warmed and cooled by the same winter and summer, as a white man is?

DONALD: I know this! I heard this on the radio, but not like that!

AMEN: *(Passionate)* If you prick us, do we not bleed? If you tickle us, do we not laugh?

AMEN: If you poison us, do we not die? And if you wrong us, shall we not revenge? If we are like you in the rest, we will resemble you in that. If a Negro wrong a white, what is his humility? Revenge. If a white man wrong a Negro, what should his sufferance be by Christian example? Why, revenge. The villany you teach me, I will execute, and it shall go hard but I will better the instruction.

*(*DONALD *and* ZENO *stare, stupefied.)*

ZENO: I hardly understood fifty percent of that.

AMEN: It's Shakespeare!

DONALD: *(Laughing)* There ain't no Negroes in Shakespeare!

AMEN: Um…*Othello*. Famously.

ZENO: Was that *Othello*?

DONALD: *The Merchant of Venice,* but ruint. Coloreds can't do Shakespeare!

AMEN: I just did!

DONALD: By changing it!

AMEN: Amen made it his own. That's good acting.

DONALD: You can't make Shakespeare stories your own. They're a thousand years old and English!

AMEN: I can tell whatever stories I want. Well or badly, that's for you to judge. But don't tell me I can't tell 'em!

ZENO: Don't know exactly what you said, but it sounded awfully good.

AMEN: Thank you, Zeno.

DONALD: But wrong.

ZENO: You ever been in any movies?

AMEN: Bunches.

DONALD: What?

AMEN: *The Girl from Chicago, Murder in Harlem, God's Stepchildren*—

ZENO: Can't say I heard of those.

DONALD: Cause they're race pictures.

AMEN: More politely called sepia pictures.

DONALD: White people never see 'em.

AMEN: Then you got some catching up to do, brother. If you like movies.

ZENO: I love movies.

AMEN: What's your favorite?

ZENO: *The Old Code*. Same writer as *Eyes of the Totem*, by the way. Did your wife meet him?

AMEN: Nobody meets the writer.

DONALD: Juarez.

ZENO: What?

DONALD: My favorite movie.

AMEN: It's terrible!

DONALD: It's got Paul Muni!

AMEN: As a Mexican!

DONALD: If you can play Shakespeare, Paul Muni can play Mexican.

ZENO: Mexican ain't a race.

AMEN: Yes, it is, Zeno! Stand up for yourself!

DONALD: It's a nationality, like American. My race is German.

ZENO: Some Mexicans look like me, some like you, some like you.

AMEN: Paul Muni don't look like no Juarez.

ZENO: That's so. Juarez was from Oaxaca, like my papa. He was dark.

DONALD: Paul Muni was still good.

AMEN: Everybody in that movie's white. Palest bunch of Mexicans ever assembled.

DONALD: Brian Aherne's gonna get the Academy Award, you just wait. Vivian met him once. Vivian met everybody.

*(*DONALD *suddenly breaks down sobbing.* AMEN *and* ZENO *stop cleaning him for a moment, puzzled.)*

ZENO: Are we hurting you, Mr Walter? We'll go gentle.

AMEN: It's the fumes. They stinging my eyes, too.

DONALD: Vivian...I'm sorry...

AMEN: *(Mouths to* ZENO*)* His wife.

ZENO: *(Mouths to* AMEN*)* But we can't talk about her.

AMEN: Brother Donald, should we call your wife? Does she know you're here?

DONALD: No!

AMEN: She's probably worried about you.

ZENO: Amen, don't—

AMEN: Don't be embarrassed—she'll want to know you're all right—

DONALD: Vivian's gone!

AMEN: She left?

DONALD: Don't talk about her—she's gone!

ZENO: Amen, shut up!

AMEN: She bound to come back when she hear what happened to you—

DONALD: She's dead! She ain't coming back! Shut the fuck up!

AMEN: Oh.

ZENO: See?

AMEN: Apologies, Brother Donald. And condolences.

ZENO: Yes, we're very sorry. *(Mouths to* AMEN*)* But shut up!

AMEN: We understand, don't we, Zeno? I think we understand everything now.

*(*DONALD *just keeps crying.)*

AMEN: You know, brother Donald, I just realized you remind me of someone. Someone in the movies. A very well-known actor, in fact.

ZENO: Amen, shhh!

AMEN: Lorenzo Tucker. Star of *Ten Minutes to Live, Temptation—*

DONALD: Never heard of him.

ZENO: Amen, that ain't gonna help!

AMEN: And *Harlem after Midnight.*

DONALD: A colored actor?!

AMEN: Not very colored. A bright mulatto like you.

DONALD: I ain't mulatto!

ZENO: Amen, shut your mouth! He's in a delicate state!

DONALD: Get me a mirror!

AMEN: He threw himself in that tar pit cause his wife died!

DONALD: I need to see my face!

ZENO: He could still be grummy! Suicidal!

*(*DONALD *cries.)*

ZENO: Look how broke up he is. He musta loved her something awful. You ever seen anyone love like that?

DONALD: I want to know what happened!

AMEN: Yeah, it's sad, but he's sobering up!

ZENO: I never cried like that in my life.

AMEN: Cause you live in a museum.

DONALD: What happened?

AMEN: He'll be okay!

ZENO: I'll get you that mirror.

DONALD: *Gracias.*

ZENO: *Habla Español?*

DONALD: *Un poquito. De puertorriqueños en Brooklyn.* [A little. From Puerto Ricans in Brooklyn.]

ZENO: You know a lot of languages!

DONALD: I pick 'em up easy.

AMEN: How did Mrs Walter pass, if I may ask?

ZENO: *(Searching for a mirror)* Amen, dammit!

DONALD: She—she—she—she—

AMEN: I see, I see. None of my beeswax.

ZENO: *(Handing* DONALD *a mirror)* Here you go.

DONALD: *(Looking in mirror)* Oh. Oh!

ZENO: You're gonna be all right.

DONALD: My face is still white.

AMEN: But the color's creeping up.

ZENO: You fell in the Tar Pits! It's slow going, but we're cleaning it off. Look!

*(*ZENO *pulls the sheet off of* DONALD*'s legs revealing that they are mostly clean of tar, only a streak or two remaining.* DONALD*'s underwear, however is still a tarry mess.)*

DONALD: Where's my dick? I can't see my dick!

AMEN: Size don't mean nothing, Brother Donald. As far as the ladies is concerned, it ain't so much the worm as the wiggle. It's somewhere in that tar ball. Hold still and we'll take care of it.

DONALD: No! Leave my dick alone!

AMEN: You can't go around with a sticky johnson.

DONALD: Don't touch it! Colored people collect white dicks!

*(*ZENO *laughs.)*

AMEN: Say what?

DONALD: And keep 'em in a dick museum.

(For once, AMEN *doesn't know what to say. He just throws* DONALD *a cloth to clean himself.* DONALD *starts cleaning his crotch.)*

DONALD: How'd I get all this tar?

ZENO: We were hoping you'd tell us.

*(*AMEN *and* ZENO *try to clean* DONALD*'s torso while he cleans his own crotch.)*

DONALD: Don't!

ZENO: You can clean your privates, but you're not gonna be able to get your back without help.

AMEN: You need dark men to make you light.

*(*DONALD *lets them clean his back and chest while he scrubs energetically at his crotch.)*

DONALD: Gotta clean, gotta get it clean.

AMEN: Go slow, brother!

DONALD: Can't get it clean, cut it off!

AMEN: Whoa!

DONALD: Cut it out!

ZENO: Don't hurt yourself Mr Walter!

DONALD: Cut out the corruption!

AMEN: Too much friction and you might ignite yourself!

DONALD: Or the whole body's destroyed!

ZENO: It's just tar, and it's coming off.

DONALD: Better destroyed than corrupted! Contaminated!

AMEN: Zeno, explain the tar! Brother Donald, listen! *(Grabs* DONALD*'s hand)*

DONALD: Contaminated beyond redemption!

AMEN: Zeno's gonna tell you about the Tar Pits, right Zeno?

DONALD: Corrupt to the core…

ZENO: Mr Walter, somehow you fell in one of the La Brea Tar Pits—

AMEN: God knows how—

ZENO: —Like prehistoric mammals did—

*(*DONALD *is starting to listen to* ZENO*.)*

ZENO: That's why they call it the Death Trap of the Ages. They got stuck.

AMEN: *(Sees* DONALD *listening)* Elaborate…

ZENO: They went to get a drink—

AMEN: And...?

ZENO: And fell in.

AMEN: Brother Donald, is that what you did? Got a drink and fell in?

DONALD: I don't...remember...

ZENO: And their bones got preserved in the tar forever, very lucky for science—

AMEN: But not so lucky for the mammoth ground tigers—

ZENO: And now we can read the bones—scientists can put them back together and learn that part of our history, ten thousand years ago. Written in a kind of code if you only know how to read it.

AMEN: And if that caretaker and those cops and firemen hadn't pulled you out, we'd be picking over your bones ten thousand years from now.

DONALD: But how'd I—?

AMEN: Lemme reconstruct this for you, Brother Donald. You had you a drink or two, I can detect by olfaction—

DONALD: I dunno, maybe.

AMEN: Now that Prohibition's over, nothing wrong with a little hooch—you had a drink—

DONALD: Okay...

AMEN: Why?

DONALD: Thirsty?

AMEN: I think you're missing your wife.

DONALD: Vivian!

ZENO: Amen, that's personal—

AMEN: I'm reconstructing a crime.

DONALD: I didn't do it! I'm innocent!

ZENO: There's no crime—an accident—

AMEN: Suicide is a crime. *(Silence)* You jump in that tar on purpose, Brother Donald? Outta depression?

DONALD: I didn't do it!

AMEN: Someone push you?

*(*DONALD *shrugs.)*

AMEN: You just jump in for fun? Think it's sexy like the black mud of Ballona Creek—?

ZENO: Amen, you're fabulizing!	DONALD: I miss Vivian!
AMEN: —Thick and dark and staining you—	DONALD: I miss her!
AMEN: Cause you wanted to join the mud people—!	DONALD: I miss my wife!

*(*ZENO *gestures for* AMEN *to be quiet. Pause)*

AMEN: *(Gently)* She been gone long, Brother Donald?

*(*DONALD *sobs.)*

AMEN: It was recent, wasn't it?

DONALD: What time is it?

ZENO: Almost nine.

DONALD: She died— *(Thinks)* —Four—

ZENO: *Dios mio!*	AMEN: Four days ago!?

DONALD: Four hours ago. Round five p.m.

AMEN: Was she sick?

DONALD: That's all I can say about it.

AMEN: She have an accident?

ZENO: Amen, he's grieving!	DONALD: Don't talk about my wife!

DONALD: *(Reaching toward his clothes)* Gimme my pants!

ZENO: Mr Walter, you can't put 'em on till you're all clean.

DONALD: *(Gets his pants)* I need—I have to— *(Goes through pockets)*

AMEN: You can't wear clothes on top of tar and kerosene—

DONALD: Where—is—?

AMEN: You're flammable!

DONALD: *(Freezes)* I'm what?

ZENO: You could catch fire. Let us finish.

DONALD: *(Sniffs)* Kerosene?

*(*AMEN *silently points to the kerosene.)*

ZENO: It's the only way we can clean you.

AMEN: Hold still.

*(*AMEN *and* ZENO *try to clean* DONALD.*)*

AMEN: I saw someone burnt up from kerosene. Weren't much left of him.

DONALD: *(Pulling away)* Don't touch my dick!

AMEN: I don't wanna touch your nasty old pecker!

(They stare at each other for a moment. Then DONALD *lifts his arms in an invitation for them to finish cleaning his arms and torso. They go to work again, in silence for a moment. Another Count Basie tune is faintly audible through the closed door.* DONALD *starts to sing. He's not bad.)*

DONALD: *(Sings)*
Mein Erbe nun [My heritage now]
nehm' ich zu eigen. [yields to the hero.]

*(*AMEN *and* ZENO *try not to let* DONALD *see their reaction, but they give each other concerned looks behind his back.*

Donald gradually gets so caught up in the aria that he begins to cry.)

DONALD:
Verfluchter Reif! [Accursed charm!]
Furchtbarer Ring! [Terrible ring!]
Dein Gold fass' ich [My hand grasps thee,]

DONALD: *Und geb' es nun fort.* [and gives thee away.]

AMEN: Brother Donald, is that German?

DONALD: *Der Wassertiefe* [Ye sisters wise]

ZENO: Of course, it's German. It's opera!

DONALD: *Weise Schwestern,* [who dwell in the waters]

AMEN: Some opera's Italian.

DONALD: *Des Rheines schwimmende Töchter,* [give ear, ye sorrowing Rhinemaids]

ZENO: He sounds like he's hawking— that's German.

DONALD: *Such dank' ich redlichen Rath*: [good counsel lives in your reeds]

AMEN: Ain't very patriotic.

DONALD: *Was ihr begehrt,* [what you desire,]

ZENO: You don't even know what he's singing.

DONALD: *Ich geb es euch:* [I leave to you:]

AMEN: We'll be at war with Germany before you know it.

DONALD: *Aus meiner Asche* [now from my ashes]

ZENO: Which is why you need to shut up and do your job.

DONALD: *Nehmt es zu eigen!* [take your treasure!]

AMEN: Maybe it ain't German.

DONALD: *Das Feuer, das mich verbrennt,* [Let fire, burning this hand]

ZENO: It's a German fat lady song.

DONALD: *Rein'ge vom Fouch den Ring!* [cleanse, too, the ring from its curse!]

AMEN: Maybe it's Yiddish.

DONALD: *Ihr in der Flut* [Ye in the flood,]

ZENO: Yiddish?

DONALD: *Löset ihn auf,* [wash it away,]

AMEN: It's Jewish German.

DONALD: *Und lauter bewahrt* [and purer preserve]

AMEN: You hear a lot of Yiddish in Hollywood.

DONALD: *Das lichte Gold,* [your shining gold] *das euch zum Unheil geraubt.* [that to your sorrow was stolen]

AMEN: You know, like Al Jolson.

DONALD: It's Wagner!

ZENO: German!

DONALD: Not Yiddish! It's Brunnhilde's Immolation.

DONALD: Vivian understudied it at the Bowl.

ZENO: It is a fat lady song!

DONALD: Vivian wasn't fat!

AMEN: Zeno, we best not be talking about Brother Donald's wife singing Nazi songs.

DONALD: Wagner died fifty years ago! He wasn't a Nazi.

AMEN: Hitler loves him.

DONALD: I'm not a Nazi! Vivian wasn't a Nazi. My mother was a Sudetenland German but she came to New York in 1894.

AMEN: Do you think the Jews started the war to make money?

ZENO: Amen, you don't think that?

AMEN: Or that F D R's real last name is Rosenveld?

DONALD: Hitler annexed Czechoslovakia to protect the Sudetenland Germans!

AMEN: I see, I see. And now he's protecting the Polacks?

DONALD: There are Germans living there!

AMEN: Are you defending Hitler?

DONALD: Germany was in trouble—he's starting over, wiping the slate clean—

AMEN: Aha! You are a Nazi! Or at least a sympathizer!

DONALD: Hollywood ain't controlled by Jews?

AMEN: Well…

DONALD: Something gets too corrupt, it's better off destroyed.

ZENO: You're almost all clean, Mr Walter.

AMEN: Yeah, you don't need to destroy yourself. Even if you did have intimate colored relations.

DONALD: I didn't!

AMEN: Did Mrs Walter?

ZENO: Dammit, Amen!

DONALD: You lying little—!

AMEN: Amen's just trying to put two and two together—she wasn't sick, it wasn't an accident—

DONALD: He killed her.

AMEN: That's what I'm getting at, Brother Donald—

DONALD: Stop calling me Brother.

ZENO: Amen, careful— AMEN: Who killed her? Did you call the police?

DONALD: He…violated her. Then cut her up and let her bleed out.

AMEN: Who? *(Silence)* A colored man? Amen can't quite make sense of this—

ZENO: Amen, the man's wife died four hours ago! He almost suicided himself in a tar pit, and you're pestering him with a mess of detectivity!

ZENO: He's drunk! He's in shock! AMEN: I'm trying to help him out! Get him justice!

ZENO: It's not our business! Probably more complicated than we can imagine—

ZENO: We don't have all the facts— AMEN: That's why I'm asking about the police!

DONALD: No! AMEN: What was his name?

AMEN: Do you know the man's name?

DONALD: *(Crying)* Some clarinetist…he had his mouth on her—

AMEN: But you know his name?

*(*DONALD *nods.)*

AMEN: Then you gotta report it— *(Heads toward a telephone)* —Colored or not, the police can find him—

DONALD: No! No police! Too late for police.

ZENO: They can't bring her back, Mr Walter, but Amen's right for once—

AMEN: Don't you want the man found?

DONALD: He can't be found! AMEN: He killed your wife!

ZENO: After you're cleaned up and sobered up we can go to the police.

ZENO: We can take you. Gotta be reported.

AMEN: He can't be found? Why can't he be found?

DONALD: I heard your plan.

ZENO: What?

AMEN: What plan?

DONALD: I was half passed out, but I heard you say you're sneaking into a whites-only club through the back door.

ZENO: Amen's plan. I'm not doing it.

AMEN: What's that have to do with—

AMEN: Oh, come on, you are, too!

DONALD: It's illegal for colored boys to go in there. If you did, I'd have to report you.

AMEN: Count Basie's playing!

DONALD: They let him in—that's the beginning.

ZENO: Amen, don't provoke him!

DONALD: Palomar Ballroom is ruint. Might as well burn it down.

AMEN: Zeno, back me up!

DONALD: You letting him lead you into trouble? Lose your job? Don't lose your job, Zeno, that's the end! I lost mine and now I got nothing.

ZENO: We're not doing it. Why are we talking about it?

AMEN: Yeah, why are we? There's a murderer loose. You gonna let that black bastard clarinetist get away with it?

(Silence)

DONALD: Then hurry up.

AMEN: Almost done.

ZENO: Just have to be careful with the kerosene. If we scratch your skin—

AMEN: Main part left is— *(Gestures)* —Your responsibility.

DONALD: You do it.

AMEN: Thought you didn't want me touching it. Scared I'd put it in the National Pale Pecker Museum.

DONALD: I was drunker then.

AMEN: Naw.

DONALD: You're the professional.

ZENO: I'll do it.

DONALD: No. *(To* AMEN*)* You.

AMEN: Fine. If I can find it. *(He proceeds to clean* DONALD*'s crotch.)*

DONALD: I am honored to have someone so well-traveled taking charge of my personal care. What'd you think of New Jersey?

AMEN: Prettier than you might think. Jersey, I mean.

DONALD: Been to Montclair?

AMEN: Beautiful sunsets.

DONALD: What train'd you take to get there?

AMEN: Oh, I don't remember.

ZENO: Who remembers trains?

DONALD: The Blue Comet!

ZENO: That one's famous!

AMEN: Naw, the Blue Comet don't stop in Montclair. It's from Elizabethport to Atlantic City.

DONALD: I stand corrected. Some Jersey Central train. What's your favorite place in Mexico?

AMEN: You spent time there, too?

DONALD: Never. But you said—

AMEN: Amen recommends Guanajuato. They got a museum of mummies.

ZENO: You don't say.

DONALD: And how'd you end up here?

AMEN: Same as you, I expect. You can be who you want in Los Angeles. Best place in the country for the Negro these days. Oh, and I wanna be in movies, like your wife.

DONALD: You been everywhere, ain't you?

AMEN: Travel's how you learn history, seeing it for yourself. History books chock full of lies.

DONALD: Everywhere the trains run.

AMEN: Hold still—Mister Johnson's almost good as new.

DONALD: Finish up quick, and I'll tip you good, George.

*(*AMEN *freezes.)*

ZENO: His name's Amen, Mr Walter.

AMEN: Like the Egyptian god.

DONALD: Could've sworn I heard your name was George. One of George Pullman's boys.

AMEN: Best not to disrespect someone's got your weewee in his hand.

DONALD: That's how you been everywhere—as a Pullman Porter!

AMEN: I quit it last year. Too many miles of smiles. *(Fake toothy grin)*

DONALD: Seem like this is a step down, polishing my knob.

AMEN: *(Stepping away from* DONALD*)* More like a button, but it's polished. You shine.

DONALD: Your pleasure, I'm sure.

AMEN: Brother Donald, we wasn't gonna tell you—

DONALD: I ain't your brother!

AMEN: In a way you are, Brother Donald. We didn't wanna hurt your feelings, but now I don't care so much about that. You been dumped.

DONALD: What do you mean?

ZENO: Amen, can it!

AMEN: Them white cops dumped you here like trash when you shoulda been at a hospital. But the white hospitals they went to all refused you, my brother. We took you into Bimini through the back door.

DONALD: *(After a moment) Necesito pantalones.* [I need pants.]

ZENO: *Sí, enseguida.* [Yes, right away.] *(He starts rummaging about.)*

AMEN: What're you talking about?

DONALD: *Y una camisa.* [And a shirt.] *(He paws through his pile of clothes.)*

ZENO: *Claro.* [Of course.]

AMEN: Talk English!

DONALD: *Y ropa interior.* [And underwear.]

AMEN: No fair speaking Spanish!

ZENO: *No encuentro nada.* [I can't find anything.]

AMEN: Am I gonna have to call the Mexican Repatriation Program?

DONALD: *(Wrapping himself in the sheet) No puedo salir a la calle desnudo!* [I can't go outside naked!]

*(*ZENO *laughs.)*

AMEN: What?

ZENO: We have to get Mr Walter some clothes. His are mostly tar.

AMEN: Lost and found?

ZENO: It's locked up this late. I thought we might have old uniforms here in storage, but—

AMEN: Here, you can have my shirt. *(He takes off his white uniform coat and shirt.)*

DONALD: I'm not wearing no—

ZENO: It's all we've got. *(He takes off his white uniform pants.)*

AMEN: Apologies, Brother Donald, but you're gonna have to go to the police dressed like the help.

(As ZENO *takes off his pants he finds the black object he put in his pocket earlier. The handkerchief is stained with blood.)*

DONALD: *(Still examining his clothes)* The hell I am!	ZENO: *Dios mio!* [My god!]

AMEN: Either that or you go outta here stinking like tar and looking like a freshly paved road.

*(*ZENO *hides the black object in the handkerchief.)*

DONALD: I ain't going to the police.

ZENO: *(Handing* DONALD *his pants)* Mr Walter, why don't you use the locker room to change?

DONALD: Where is it?

*(*AMEN *points to the locker room and hands* DONALD *his shirt.)*

AMEN: Over there. Nobody in it at this hour.

DONALD: I'm gonna need some shoes. *(He disappears through the interior door.)*

AMEN: I ain't giving that paddy my shoes. We got any pool sandals?

ZENO: Might be some in the— *(Gestures)*

AMEN: *(Rummaging, finds sandals)* Let's get him out of here before Amen kick his ass—

ZENO: *(Shows* AMEN *the black object)* Amen, what's this look like to you?

AMEN: *(Comes over, looks)* Oh, no. I ain't touching that.

ZENO: It was in Mr Walter's pants pocket.

AMEN: Damn!

ZENO: Is it—? It didn't look right, but then it bled—

AMEN: Pretty sure.

ZENO: It was *in his pocket*!

AMEN: Sometimes folks take justice into their own hands, then take…souvenirs.

ZENO: He won't go to the police.

AMEN: And this why that black man can't be found.

ZENO: It's all that's left of him.

AMEN: Fuck.

ZENO: What do we do, Amen?

AMEN: We can't take this to the police ourselves.

ZENO: They'll think we did it.

AMEN: And killed Mrs. Walter.

ZENO: *Ay, dios mio!*

AMEN: Where's that knife?

*(*DONALD *reappears dressed in the uniform they gave him.)*

DONALD: Gimme my clothes and I'll go.

*(*AMEN *and* ZENO *stand frozen.)*

DONALD: I'm sobered up. You find me any shoes?

*(*AMEN *throws the sandals at* DONALD*.)*

ZENO: Amen!

DONALD: *(Putting on the sandals)* That ain't so hospitable. Thought Mr Pullman trained you better than that, George.

AMEN: Zeno, I feel I'm no longer under any obligation to speak to Mr Walter. Can't tell him nothing.

DONALD: I don't care that you do—I'm on my way out.

ZENO: Amen, at least hold it together till he's gone.

AMEN: Mr Walter is indeed on his way out, which is why I got nothing to say to him. He's had his day, he no longer counts.

ZENO: Mr Walter, I can take you on the streetcar to the police.

AMEN: With no pants?

DONALD: Ain't going to the cops. I'm going home.

AMEN: Zeno, I don't believe we should permit Mr Walter to take his leave.

DONALD: Can't stop me.

AMEN: For his own safety he oughta stay a bit longer.

DONALD: *(To* ZENO*)* Help me pack up my clothes so I can burn 'em.

*(*ZENO *reluctantly helps* DONALD *gather the tar-stained clothes.)*

AMEN: Zeno, has Mr Walter taken a shower or a dip in our famous plunge?

DONALD: Your friend got a weird way of talking.

AMEN: Amen suspect he's still covered in kerosene. Yes, I detect that through olfaction.

DONALD: I'll shower at home.

ZENO: Mr. Walter, you really do need to tell the police what happened.

AMEN: Zeno, you and me and Bimini Baths will be liable if we let him walk out of here combustible. I seen a man burnt by kerosene.

ZENO: One of your fabulations—

AMEN: Mr. Walter might wish to hear me fabulate for his own edification.

ZENO: Edification!

DONALD: I don't need no—

AMEN: The burning weren't the worst of it, though.

DONALD: *Habla demasiado!* [He talks too much!]

ZENO: What was?

AMEN: The reason for it.

DONALD: What?

AMEN: A woman.

DONALD: I definitely don't need—

ZENO: What'd she do?

AMEN: She loved him. Ain't that always the way?

DONALD: *(Starts to leave)* Don't talk about women! My wife is dead!

AMEN: *(Blocks* DONALD*'s way)* She loved him and his music. His clarinet.

DONALD: Clarinet?!

AMEN: Weren't nobody in Northern California could play like he did.

AMEN: You know Dunsmuir, Zeno, in the shadow of Mount Shasta? Clarinetist used to play there in a bootleg band for the loggers and the ladies. One of them ladies fell for him and his ebony instrument. She weren't exactly a quiff but not on the level, neither. Fed her husband a line for a couple of months before he caught on—

*(*DONALD *tries to leave, but* AMEN *lights his cigarette lighter and blocks* DONALD*'s way with the flame.)*

ZENO: Amen, goddammit!

*(*DONALD *stops.)*

AMEN: Central Pacific Railroad stop right there in Dunsmuir, so I seen it with my own eyes. Be surprised what George see when you don't see him. Husband finds out and that's the end of the big band sound in Dunsmuir, no more swinging 'cept on a tree. Cause this clarinetist, this cat who made music with the wrong chick, he had him the privilege of color. So not just the husband, but the whole town came out to see justice done, couple thousand in the crowd. Some enterprising folks selling lemonade, whisky, deviled eggs to those watching the show. Took 'em hours, train even waited so the Pullman passengers could participate, iffen they wish.

*(*AMEN *closes the lighter.)*

ZENO: When was this? Long time ago!

AMEN: I told you I saw it. Three years ago. Amen was on that train. I heard a man screaming, saw him dangling, heard them laughing, saw them cut him down and douse him with— *(Points to the kerosene)* — Till he smell like Mr Walter, stinking all the way to the station where me and all the other Georges was hid, cause colored folk don't wanna be anywhere near a riled-up mob like that.

DONALD: It ain't true! We'd a heard about it!

AMEN: Papers don't report this shit, specially when it happen to a dark man in a town so small he could be dragged from one end to the other behind a Model A in less than a minute, flaming and hollering all the way, cause the noose only did half the job. On the second lap the Ford pause long enough for the husband—inspired by the jeering crowd—to stick a knife in the fire and turn that squirming, screaming man into a woman. "Souvenir!" the crowd shouted.

DONALD: No!

AMEN: "Souvenir! Souvenir!"

DONALD: This…didn't… happen!

AMEN: Couldn't tell what killed him in the end:

AMEN: Hangin', draggin', burnin' or cuttin', but bout ten minutes later the clarinetist no longer make a sound, except the scrape of his corpse on the gravel and the— *(Makes a whoosh sound)* —Of the kerosene flames as the Model A go by. At every pass there was less of him. When the Ford finally crawled to a stop, the mad noise of the crowd fell silent, cause there weren't nothing left but a black, smoking torso at the husband's feet and the smell of kerosene barbecue. He look down at the clarinetist, up at the mob. They look back at him. "He kilt her!" No response. "Nigger kilt my wife!" Silence. Husband realize the crowd ain't looking at him. Something coming down the street behind him. He turn, knife in one hand, the musician's "instrument" in the other. "He ain't kilt me," wife say, big as life, staring in her husband's eyes, "He loved me."

DONALD: You a liar.

AMEN: I seen what I seen.

DONALD: None of this happened! You made it up!

ZENO: She wasn't dead!

DONALD: He didn't play the fucking clarinet!

AMEN: Why would I make that shit up?

AMEN: Anyways, that ain't the end of the story. Wife say "He loved me." Husband jump on her quick as shit and stab her in her nigger-loving heart.

DONALD: You—motherfucking—fairy—!

AMEN: Now, that kinda a contradiction in terms—

ZENO: He stabbed his wife?

DONALD: I did not! She—

ZENO: What happened then? Did the mob turn on him?

AMEN: Nobody move. They too frozen by their own crime to stop his. Off he run.

ZENO: He get away?

AMEN: Nobody move, 'cept the Pullman Porters. Nobody notice all them Georges, silent, smiling, slipping off the train. Nobody notice them Georges sneakin' back on the train ten minutes later. Nobody notice the husband never found.

ZENO: The Negro stick together.

AMEN: 'Cept that clarinetist—he weren't Negro.

ZENO: No?

AMEN: Mexican.

DONALD: *(After a moment)* Outta my way.

AMEN: *(Clicking lighter on)* Amen don't believe Vivian hated clarinet at all.

DONALD: Don't say her name!

AMEN: Amen think you hate clarinet 'cause Vivian loved her some clarinet. Put her mouth on it, her angel kiss—

DONALD: You don't know nothing about her.	AMEN: Ain't no violation if she kissed him back.

DONALD: You know nothing about me!

AMEN: We know every inch of your tar-stained body, don't we Zeno? Like any body servant knows the filth he cleans.

DONALD: I didn't touch neither of 'em!

AMEN: *(Clicks off the lighter)* Zeno, what you got there in your hanky?

ZENO: Aw, Amen—

AMEN: Show Mr Walter what you found. He thinks we don't know nothin'.

ZENO: *(Opening the handkerchief)* I don't think it's really—I mean—it could be—

DONALD: Where'd you get that?

AMEN: I think you know where, Brother Donald.

DONALD: Where?!

ZENO: Your pants pocket.

DONALD: Don't mean nothing.

AMEN: Ain't the worm but the wiggle.

DONALD: Step aside.

AMEN: Or?

*(*DONALD *produces the switchblade.)*

AMEN: Third time's the charm.

ZENO: Don't act like that, Mr. Walter. You're in enough trouble.

AMEN: And then gotta bop Zeno, eliminate the witness. Ain't that right, Zeno?

ZENO: I got you, Amen.

DONALD: You taking orders from this gunsel?

AMEN: Who you calling a gunsel?

AMEN: You ain't performing with politeness.

DONALD: Ain't you the boss?

ZENO: He's the one figured out what you did.

DONALD: *Es pura mierda! Esta mintiendo!* [He's making shit up! Lying to you!]

ZENO: *Él está diciendo la verdad!* [He's telling the truth!]

AMEN: Spiggoty English!

ZENO: *¿La tuviste te matar?* [Did you have to kill her?]

AMEN: English, Zeno, English!

DONALD: *(Starting to cry, hysterical) Me mató primero!* [She killed me first!]

AMEN: You the gunsel!

DONALD: *Me rompió el corazón!* [She broke my heart!]

AMEN: You the fairy whose wife run off with the clarinetist!

DONALD: *Ella me amaba a mi, no a un nigger sucio!* [She was supposed to love me, not a dirty nigger!]

AMEN: Making me clean your nasty dick! That's what you want! You want black dick so bad you cut you one! This what you want?!

*(*AMEN *grabs* DONALD *and kisses on the mouth, hard, brutal.* DONALD *pushes free, swipes at* AMEN *with the knife.)*

AMEN: You the nigger!

DONALD: Corruption! Contamination! *(He grabs the kerosene and splashes some on his mouth, frantically scrubbing.)*

ZENO: Amen, you lost your mind?

AMEN: I see, I see! Gotta purge, gotta burn the black out!

ZENO: Now I gotta fire you for sure!

DONALD: That's what he did to her! And she let him!

DONALD: I ain't letting you!

*(*DONALD *comes toward* AMEN *with the knife.* AMEN *clicks on the lighter.)*

AMEN: Get near enough to cut me, you go up in flame.

*(*AMEN *and* DONALD *freeze.)*

ZENO: *(Carefully)* Mr Walter, we understand you love Mrs Walter very much.

DONALD: Yes...

AMEN: Too much. She some kinda whore.

ZENO: And I know that feeling can take over your heart so there's nothing else left.

DONALD: Nothing.

ZENO: So when you saw her kissing someone else, you lost the last thing you had.

DONALD: Nothing left.

ZENO: You're at zero. You cried yourself to nothing.

AMEN: He ain't at zero, he at negative something!

ZENO: So you need to go before worse happens.

AMEN: Zeno, we can't let him go! He kilt two people already!

DONALD: You got the flame, I got the fuel. *(Gestures with kerosene can)* Lemme douse ya!

AMEN: You fling that kerosene on me and we all burn. The whole bath house!

(After a tense moment of stand-off, ZENO *suddenly rushes toward* DONALD*, then swerves and tackles* AMEN *instead, knocking him into the Dictaphone, which starts playing back their earlier recording. The lighter goes flying.)*

AMEN: Zeno, you sonovabitch!

ZENO ON DICTAPHONE: *Hola, buenas dias...*

ZENO: Mr Walter, run!

ZENO ON DICTAPHONE: *Este es Zenobio Remedios—*

ZENO: Get outta here!

ZENO ON DICTAPHONE: No!

AMEN: I'll light him! I'll light you!

ZENO ON DICTAPHONE: *Mi nombre es Zeno—*

(As they wrestle, DONALD *dodges past them, still carrying the kerosene, and opens the exterior door. The clarinet solo section in One O'Clock Jump pours in through the door.* DONALD *freezes, listening.)*

ZENO: I can't hold him long!

ZENO ON DICTAPHONE: Zeno the beanbag.

AMEN: You can't hold me at all!

ZENO ON DICTAPHONE: Amen, I'm trying to—

AMEN ON DICTAPHONE: Zeno the greaser.

DONALD: That fucking clarinet!

*(*DONALD*, still clutching the can of kerosene, darts into the fight and picks up the lighter.* AMEN *and* ZENO *crash into him, knocking him down. The knife falls from his hand.* DONALD *abandons the knife, takes the lighter and kerosene, runs out the door, slams it behind himself and disappears.)*

ZENO ON DICTAPHONE: Shut up, you damn—

AMEN ON DICTAPHONE: Say it!

ZENO ON DICTAPHONE: No!

AMEN ON DICTAPHONE: Spic.

*(*AMEN *and* ZENO *wrestle, a struggle that echoes their earlier dance, each trying to dominate the other. It's desperate and rough.* DONALD *is forgotten. Without being overtly sexual, the intensity is passionate, frightening. The fight escalates as the Dictaphone plays.)*

ZENO ON DICTAPHONE: Shhh!

AMEN ON DICTAPHONE: Spic.

ZENO ON DICTAPHONE: Spook.

AMEN ON DICTAPHONE: Wetback.

ZENO ON DICTAPHONE: Spade.

AMEN ON DICTAPHONE: Pachuco.

ZENO ON DICTAPHONE: Dinge.

AMEN ON DICTAPHONE: Mojado.

ZENO ON DICTAPHONE: Golliwog.

AMEN ON DICTAPHONE: Aw! Spiggoty!

ZENO ON DICTAPHONE: *(Laughs)* Spiggoty?

AMEN ON DICTAPHONE: Spiggoty English?

ZENO ON DICTAPHONE: Chango!

AMEN ON DICTAPHONE: Chango?

ZENO ON DICTAPHONE: Spiggoty Spanish, eight ball?

AMEN ON DICTAPHONE: Beaner!

ZENO ON DICTAPHONE: You said that already. I win.

AMEN ON DICTAPHONE: I said beanbag.

*(*AMEN *gains the upper hand, pins* ZENO, *who continues to struggle. They grunt and groan.* ZENO*'s groans rise to a terrified moan, a strange, horrifying sound.)*

ZENO ON DICTAPHONE: Maroon!

AMEN ON DICTAPHONE: Border nigger.

ZENO ON DICTAPHONE: You said it! I win.

ZENO: *(Panicked) Esto no es lo que quiero! ¡No entiendo! ¡Es lo que tu quieres! Yo no!* [That's not what I want! I don't understand! This is what you want! I don't want it!]

AMEN ON DICTAPHONE: Amen used a modifier, an *adjective.* It ain't the same. Mojo.

*(*ZENO*'s panic frightens* AMEN, *who lets him up.)*

AMEN: Shit, Zeno!

*(*ZENO *leaps to his feet, grabs the knife, and points it at* AMEN*, trembling. They stare at each other, confused, angry, both breathing hard. Another stand-off)*

AMEN ON DICTAPHONE: Coon, buck, July ham?

ZENO ON DICTAPHONE: Smoked Irish!

AMEN ON DICTAPHONE: Chihuahua!

ZENO ON DICTAPHONE: Chihuahua?

AMEN ON DICTAPHONE: Shine, haunt, blue gum?

ZENO ON DICTAPHONE: Blue gum?

AMEN ON DICTAPHONE: If you get bit by a Negro with blue gums, you die. Thirty- Eighth Streeter! *(Pause)* Say it!

ZENO ON DICTAPHONE: I'm not saying—

AMEN ON DICTAPHONE: Go on, say it!

*(*AMEN *slaps the Dictaphone, which shuts it off. Silence for a moment, not even music from the Ballroom.)*

AMEN: Nothing.

ZENO: What?

AMEN: We could stop a murdering sonovabitch and instead we do nothing.

ZENO: He had a knife!

AMEN: And you ask how he feels about cutting up his wife. Feelings don't mean shit if you do nothing. I got feelings all my life, which is why I move, why I do. You do nothing. You let him go. Nothing.

ZENO: If I didn't let him go, he'da cut you. That's something.

(In the silence, a woman's scream from next door.)

AMEN: Listen to them whooping it up. We should be there.

ZENO: Don't hear the Count.

AMEN: Let's get cleaned up. I got white all over me. Then we go to the cops. You see my lighter?

(Some shouts from next door. Green and blue light is mingled with a little orange. Still no music)

ZENO: Who they gonna believe we walk in with *una verga sangrienta*? [a bloody dick].

AMEN: They believe us if we talk fucking English!

ZENO: You fabulized that whole lynching story didn't you?

AMEN: You familiar with *Hamlet*?

ZENO: That a movie?

AMEN: Hamlet fabulizes a whole play—

AMEN: —Called The Mousetrap, and tricks—	ZENO: You fabulized it! Good!

ZENO: Cause if that story's true, I'm still stuck in a room with a murderer. You one of them Georges who disappeared that husband?

AMEN: *(Smiles)* Air of mystery.

*(*ZENO *lowers the knife and starts tidying up. Sound of breaking glass next door and the blue and green light disappears, only orange remaining. Another shout and a scream.)*

AMEN: Damn! What are we missing?

*(*AMEN *opens the door. Orange light pours in, sound of roaring flames.)*

ZENO: All right, we can go to the police after we clean up.

AMEN: Naw.

ZENO: Amen, I'm agreeing with you!

AMEN: Naw!

ZENO: I get it! It's the right thing to do!

*(*AMEN *drags* ZENO *to the doorway into the orange light. They both stare for a moment. More shouts and screams. Sirens)*

AMEN: Brother Donald set fire to the Palomar Ballroom!

ZENO: With our kerosene!

AMEN: We gotta go help!

ZENO: No!

AMEN: Count Basie's in there!

ZENO: They're gonna think we did it! He used our kerosene! And your lighter!

AMEN: The whole building's coming down!

ZENO: And we got his *verga*! [dick]

AMEN: I can't hide here! People need help!

ZENO: White people!

AMEN: White people and Count Basie and his Orchestra and the kitchen staff!

(Breaks free) Hiding here ain't right!

ZENO: Go on! Get yourself kilt!

AMEN: It ain't right! Can't just do *nothing*!

*(*AMEN *disappears through the door, leaving* ZENO *standing alone in the orange light, holding the bloody handkerchief and the knife.)(Sirens, shouts, roaring flames.* ZENO *suddenly bursts into sobs. Tears run down his face as he stares at the burning building and after* AMEN. *His grief grows almost as violent as* DONALD'*s, as violent as* ZENO'*s fight with* AMEN, *then:)*

ZENO: It's not…nothing.

END OF PLAY

www.ingramcontent.com/pod-product-compliance
Lightning Source LLC
Chambersburg PA
CBHW070027110426
42741CB00034B/2666
* 9 7 8 0 8 8 1 4 5 7 9 1 9 *